Pastoring

Joe McKeever

Parson's Porch Books

www.parsonsporchbooks.com

Pastoring

ISBN: Softcover 978-1-951472-24-5

Copyright © 2019 by Joe McKeever

All rights reserved. No part of this book may be reproduced or transmitted in any form or by any means, electronic or mechanical, including photocopying, recording, or by any information storage and retrieval system, without permission in writing from the publisher.

To my big brother Ron. You have pastored churches for nearly sixty years, always with a sense of holiness and commitment. You are everything I hope to be when I grow up.

Contents

INTRODUCTION 7

CHAPTER ONE 9
  Pastor Be a Writer.

CHAPTER TWO 19
  The Hardest, Best Thing for a Preacher to Do

CHAPTER THREE 30
  When the Preacher is a Joke--and How to Prevent that from Happening

CHAPTER FOUR 36
  Fear Has No Place In The Ministry

CHAPTER FIVE 42
  "My Pastor's Not Always Right, But He's Never in Doubt."

CHAPTER SIX 50
  The Pastor's Comeuppance

CHAPTER SEVEN 58
  The Apostle Paul's Gift to Preachers

CHAPTER EIGHT 66
  You Meet the Strangest People

CHAPTER NINE 72
  What To Do When A Sermon Is Even Boring The Preacher

CHAPTER TEN 78
> How To Write Boring Articles And Preach Dull Sermons

CHAPTER ELEVEN 86
> Pastor, Take Care of Your People

CHAPTER TWELVE 93
> Someone Is Always On Deck, Pastor

Final Words 96

About The Author 97

INTRODUCTION

I suppose some books are more intentional than others. But this may be the least intentional of any book you'll ever read. It's an accident, actually.

What happened was I was combing through our website in search of articles written over the years trying to assemble a book on church health. I kept stumbling across things I'd written on pastoring, a subject I know a little about--and have the scars to prove --having devoted over forty years to serving six churches. Sometimes I would read one of the pieces and think, "That's a keeper. That would make a good book for pastors."

Gradually, I began moving the articles into a Word file, arranging them in some kind of order and editing out redundancies, deleting dated references, and correcting typos. You hold in your hand the result.

Then I wrestled with what to name this child. A title like "Pastor, Be Yourself" doesn't really say anything. Is anyone not himself? How about "Help--I'm a Pastor!" which is a variation on our book "Help! I'm a Deacon!" Or maybe "Pastoral Stuff" or "How to Pastor."

Nah. There had to be something better.

After praying about it over a few days, I came across a review of Robert Caro's latest book telling how he researches and writes his best-selling biographies on political figures. "Working" was his title.

I ordered the book.

It occurred to me that "Pastoring" is as good a title as any. That's certainly what these dozen chapters are all about.

Some years back while in a crisis of leadership in our church, one that resulted in my leaving and being, shall we say, between churches for a solid year, my wife and I claimed God's promise to us in Psalm 66. Sometime later, situated in the next pastorate, I was re-reading that Psalm. That's when I noticed it mentioned paying my vows. Until then, we had given no thought to making a vow of any kind.

So, out of gratitude for the Lord bringing us through that valley and into "a place of abundance" (Psalm 66:12), we made three vows of gratitude to the Heavenly Father: We would live simply, give generously, and encourage pastors.

These days--the summer of 2019--I've just completed ten years of retirement ministry. Much of it has been spent, I'm happy to say, in encouraging the Lord's ministers in one way or the other.

We pray this little volume will be one of those ways.

CHAPTER ONE

Pastor Be a Writer.

This will be written for the generation to come, that a people yet to be created may praise the Lord. --Psalm 102:18

I love books. I've been known to buy a book just for its title. A volume on Hollywood screenwriting was titled "Hello, he lied." A book on Christians' interaction with the world carried the excellent title "How the Church can minister to the world without losing itself." I also liked "I don't have faith enough to be an atheist."

I'm also a sucker for a great beginning of a book.

Here is how Kelly Gallagher kicked off his outstanding work *Teaching Adolescent Writers*:

You're standing in a large field minding your own business when you hear rumbling sounds in the distance. The sounds begin to intensify, and at first you wonder if it is thunder you hear approaching. Because it's a beautiful, cloudless day you dismiss this notion. As the rumbling sound grows louder, you begin to see a cloud of dust rising just over the ridge a few yards in front of you. Instantly, you become panicked because at that exact moment it dawns on you that the rumbling, you're hearing is the sound of hundreds of wild bulls stampeding over the ridge. There are hordes of them, and they are bearing down right on top of you. They are clearly faster than you and there is no time to escape. What should you do? Survival experts recommend only one of the following actions:

A) Lying down and curling up, covering your head with your arms.

B) Running directly at the bulls, screaming wildly and flailing your arms in an attempt to scare them in another direction

C) Turning and running like heck in the same direction the bulls are running (even though you know you can't outrun them)

D) Standing completely still; they'll see you and run around you

E) Screaming bad words at your parents for insisting on a back-to-nature vacation in Wyoming

Gallagher, who teaches high school in Anaheim, California, says experts recommend C. "Your only option is to run alongside the stampede to avoid being trampled."

Then, being the consummate teacher, he applies the great attention-grabbing beginning: "My students are threatened by a stampede—a literacy stampede."

He adds, "If students are going to have a fighting chance of running with the bulls, it is obvious that their ability to read and write effectively will play a pivotal role."

Illinois high school teacher Judy Allen, wife of Pastor Jim Allen of Palmyra, gave me her copy of Gallagher's book when she saw how fascinated I was with it. I'm grateful.

As the grandfather of eight intelligent, wonderful young adults, I am most definitely interested in their being able to "run with the bulls." But my concern here is for pastors and other church leaders who are trying to find their greatest effectiveness.

By the way, did you notice that I was reading and enjoying a book titled "Teaching Adolescent Writers"? I've been writing all my life and was first published in a national magazine 48 years ago. But I'm still learning.

You too? Good. Don't ever quit.

I hear preachers say, "When I retire, I'm going to go to the mountains (or the beach) and write my memoirs."

I think (but do not say), "No, you're not. If you're not writing now, you will not suddenly become a writer when you retire."

If you ever plan to write a book, get started writing now.

Not necessarily "get started writing your book," but just start writing. Write something! And do it every day.

Sometime around 1996, Minister of Education Jim Lancaster installed a computer in my office. He did it without being asked. As he plugged it in, Jim simply said, "Pastor, you're going to be needing this."

He was so right. That one act from a friend changed my life and, if I'm allowed to say, has influenced a lot of the Lord's people toward greater service. You hold in your hand one result of his gracious act.

Writing is a remarkable thing. Almost magical even.

In a 1994 article in Christianity Today, Philip Yancey notes just how remarkable it is.

In a scene from the movie "Black Robe," a Jesuit missionary tries to persuade a Huron chief to let him teach the tribe to read and write. The chief sees no benefit to this practice of scratching marks on paper until the Jesuit gives him a demonstration. "Tell me something I don't know," he says. The chief thinks for a moment and replies, "My woman's mother died in snow last winter."

The Jesuit writes a sentence and walks a few yards over to his colleague, who glances at it and then says to the chief, "Your mother-in-law died in a snowstorm?" The chief jumps back in alarm. He has just encountered the magical power of writing, which allows knowledge to be transferred in silence through symbols.

Pastor let us transfer some knowledge in symbols. And let us get on with it. The stampede is bearing down on us.

These days, in my retirement mode, in addition to cartooning for Baptist Press and accepting every speaking opportunity I can, I write. I write for my blog (www.joemckeever.com), write a column for each issue of Deacon Magazine for Lifeway, write for SBC's Facts & Trends, and other publications.

I love to write, and I really, really love to read good writing.

What I do not enjoy is reading bad writing. My wife is a career teacher of college students. From time to time, she will show me a jaw-dropping essay from some student. Rarely, the writing is outstanding, but more often, it's embarrassingly bad.

I've taught on the seminary level and was distressed at the poor mastery of the English language by these present- and future-pastors and missionaries.

It is not a revelation to say we are raising a generation of ministers who need help in learning to write effectively. As far as I can tell, the only ones who are getting help are those who take the initiative themselves to learn the craft.

Consider this as one tiny step in the direction of encouraging ministers to learn to write well.

1. Minister, start writing today. Write some every day.

Pastor Mike Miller of Jacksonville, Texas has an internet column he calls "Ask Mike." People pose religious questions to him and he responds. It's a great way to reach out to seekers, he says, also a good way to sharpen his writing and an effective way to connect with his people.

In 1990, years before Jim installed that computer, I started keeping a journal. I took a wordless book, wrote the date at the top, and proceeded to write down what was going on in my unemployed life then. (I figured the day would come when I would wonder what was going on in my mind in that period between churches.)

I kept the journal for the entire decade of the Nineties, eventually filling over fifty volumes. Mostly, it collects dust, but once in a while I pull one out and read it, laugh at stories of my grandchildren, and decide to re-use a story or sermon illustration recorded there.

Keeping that journal enabled me to "find my voice." Only by writing a great deal can one find the mode of expression that works best, that feels comfortable, and which, when you read it, you decide, "Yep. That's him."

2. Read a great deal. Nothing helps your writing like reading.

Even if you do not pay attention to the way an author writes, even if you speed through the book studying its ideas and not the style of expression, you will still develop a sense for when something is written well and when it's not.

And, since you are intent on learning to write more effectively, when you find yourself reading something particularly impressive, you will want to pause and study how the writer did what he did.

Gradually, little by little, if you continue writing some every day, your writing will improve.

3. You have been handed great tools for expression unheard of by your grandparents.

Even if you have no idea how to go online or start a blog and no desire to do so, you can buy a laptop and start writing. Write your sermons, record your thoughts, keep a journal.

Why use a computer? Why not pick up a pen and open a notebook and get started in the time-honored way of our past generations? Answers: you can do so much more with a computer and do it infinitely faster and more easily.

Editing something you have written is difficult when you pick up a sheet of paper on which you have scribbled something. You take your pen in hand, mark through some lines, insert words here and there, draw arrows to this phrase and that notation, and soon you have a royal mess.

But not with a computer.

With a computer, you "cut and paste." You highlight a section you want to move, click on "cut" and then go to the spot where you wish to set it down and insert it. Right-click the mouse and then, click on "paste," and lo and behold, you have it. Go back and delete that portion from the prior spot. Now, wasn't that easy.

Do that once and you will wonder why you waited so long to get started on computers.

4. From the first, make up your mind to edit your stuff. Otherwise, forget it.

At first, just try to get your thoughts down "on paper," as we say. Don't fret over the details. But, then, a day or more later, come back and read what you wrote and make it better and stronger.

Kelly Gallagher recommends the STAR method of editing: SUBSTITUTE some words, TAKE out others, ADD in other places, and REARRANGE some things you wrote.

Any writer will tell you that writing itself is not hard; editing is hard. Successful writers work at editing what they have written. If you are not willing to edit what you have put down on paper, you are opting for mediocrity.

Those who do not edit will have obvious errors of the kind which we all commit when in a hurry. We leave out a word, type a sound-alike word instead of the one we meant, use a plural verb with a singular subject, that sort of thing. By simply going over what we wrote a day later, we can turn out our best efforts.

Question: Do you have time to write, and time to edit?

I know the answer to that.

You do.

Each of us has 24 hours in every day, 168 hours in every week. We have as much time as anyone else and all the time we need. We have time to do those things which are really important to us.

Toward the end of his column, Philip Yancey confesses:

"I became a writer, I believe, because of my own experience of the power of words. I saw that spoiled words, their original meaning wrung out, could be reclaimed. I saw that writing could find its way into the crevices, bringing spiritual oxygen to people trapped in air-tight boxes. I saw that when God conveyed to us the essence of his self-expression, God called it the Word. The Word comes in the most freedom-enhancing way imaginable."

Study that paragraph. It's great writing. It's powerful theology. And if I'm any judge, it's encouragement to those called to be shepherds of the Lord's people to write.

Now, I'm going to let you in on a little secret: Yancey did not write that paragraph that way the first time. He labored over it. At first, he jotted down the gist of it, and may have said something about "spoiled words" and "people trapped in air-tight boxes." When he came back the next day to improve on it, he picked up on those images and decided to strengthen them. And—I'm just guessing here—it was not until the third or fourth look at what he'd written that this paragraph attained its final form.

That's how assembling words together on a page may become great writing.

In one of his books, John Piper observes that books do not change people's lives, paragraphs do. And in some cases, he says, it's sentences that change people's lives. Or even, just a word.

Such power words have.

They said of Job, "Your words have upheld him who was stumbling. Your words have stood men on their feet." (Job 4:4)

Pastoring

What do your words do, minister of (ahem) The Word?

To influence your generation, be a writer.

To influence future generations, be a good writer.

CHAPTER TWO

The Hardest, Best Thing for a Preacher to Do

Malcolm Gladwell was speaking at a forum in New York City soon. The promotion describes him thusly:

The Canadian-born 'New Yorker' staff writer Malcolm Gladwell is the author of such best-selling books as "The Tipping Point," "Blink," "Outliers," and "What the Dog Saw." Gladwell is known for taking a unique perspective on seemingly well understood topics and generating new patterns of thought about them. This provocative thinker joins Luminato to share his latest brainstorm.

Do you ever read a sentence and a day later, it's still with you, hounding your steps, disturbing your sleep, probing your spirit? That's what that description of what Gladwell did to me.

He takes seemingly well understood topics and generates new patterns of thought about them.

Anyone who can do that—who can show us a different perspective on something we thought we knew well and then can draw fascinating conclusions from it—that is someone I want to know.

You probably already know Malcolm Gladwell. Many of my friends cannot wait for his latest books and snap them up as they hit the bookstores. There's something about his unique way of looking at things that produces "aha!" moments and leaves readers gasping, "Why didn't I think of that?"

In "The Tipping Point," Gladwell wrote about how little things can make a big difference. What turns an unusual clothing item into a hot new fashion trend? What are the forces at work to cause strange shoes to go from being oddities worn only by oddballs one day to (ahem) Birkenstocks the next?

Gladwell tries to find the precise act when that change occurs. He calls that moment the tipping point.

In "Blink: The Power of Thinking Without Thinking," Gladwell focuses on intuition. Far from being a glorified hunch, he says intuition is the result of long hours of work and searching and concentration. His examples are worth the price of the book.

In "Outliers: The Story of Success," Gladwell examines achievers for what they have in common. He says we should not ask "what are these achievers like?" but "where are they from?" That is, what went into making them different from the rest of us? He finds commonalities for them.

Okay, pastor. Let's talk about you.

Malcolm Gladwell is your new role model from now on. Go forth and do with your ministry what he does with the mundane things of everyday life.

Look at the elements of your work you know backwards and forwards and see what you might

have missed. What have you overlooked because of its familiarity?

As the pastor of a church, what are the components of your work? The answer would include all of the Bible with its stories and teachings, your theological education past and present, the daily tasks of study and planning, administration and ministry, the books and magazines you read, the conferences you attend, and such.

Now, think about their interconnectedness. Their interrelatedness. What they have in common, how they fit together, what each says to the other.

Hard to do? That's too big a chore for most of us who are not used to trying to get our minds around such a gargantuan subject.

So, let's narrow it down. Next step.

Pay attention the next time a scripture story takes hold of your imagination and will not turn it loose.

That's one of the ways the Holy Spirit draws our attention to a text in which He wishes to teach/instruct/lead/convict us.

I've actually had a passage of Scripture make me angry. While reading a psalm, one verse in particular seemed to jump out at me. I spoke out loud, "That's stupid. What does that mean?" A few minutes later, in my prayer time, the Spirit opened that verse and showed how it was the very answer to the burden that had driven me to scripture-searching and prayer in the first place.

The Lord drew my attention to that text by making me angry. (A poor reflection on my spirituality, I reluctantly admit.)

Usually the way it works with me, however, is I'm intrigued by a text or Bible story. I will read it and think, "That is fascinating. Wonder why that's in the Bible?" I continue reflecting on it for days, treating it like a Rubik's Cube, turning it over and over, trying to unlock its mysteries.

Gradually, it hits me. The sealed door opens up. The mystery is made clear. Choose your metaphor.

The Lord was wanting to show me something about ministry or life in that passage. As it began to unfold, it was exhilarating.

Now, as you reflect on all that story or text contains, ask what other applications it contains.

Do the principles in that story apply elsewhere? Can you think of people in the Bible who illustrate that same lesson but in a different way? Anyone illustrate its opposite effect?

This is not the work of an afternoon. From start to finish, the entire process may take weeks or even months. However, the finished product will be life/ministry-changing and will be part of who you are from then on.

All right. Here's how that happened to me....

I found myself intrigued by the story of Asahel, nephew of King David (II Samuel 2:12-23). The younger brother of David's generals Abishai and Joab, he is described as "fleet-footed as a gazelle."

Civil war is raging throughout Israel as the son of the late King Saul, Ishbosheth, and his supporters are fighting David for the throne. A battle took place at "the pool of Gibeon." By the end of the day, David's men were victorious. If anyone was killed, we're not told.

Now, the battle over, everyone left for home. That's when Asahel comes up with his bright idea.

Like a lot of young people, he seems to have been impatient with the older generation. They moved too slowly for him. Asahel analyzed the situation and decided–correctly, I think–that if Ishbosheth's general, Abner, were taken out of the picture, the rebellion would cease. So, he decided to take care of that little problem.

The rest of the story tells how Asahel pursued Abner up the hillside intending to kill him. However–and this is fascinating–the youth was without weapons or armor (2:21). How he expected to kill Abner is anyone's guess.

Several times Abner tried to talk Asahel out of his suicidal foolishness. But his mind was made up. He would become a hero today.

When finally Asahel reached Abner, the old veteran warrior apparently never even turned around. He thrust backward with his spear, it entered the soft part of Asahel's body and exited out the back. The youth bled to death on the spot.

It's a tragic story. And, as I say, it captivated me. That's how I knew the Lord had something there for me.

Instead of Asahel inspiring his countrymen the way his uncle David had done years ago in defeating Goliath, the story says, "whenever anyone came to the spot where Asahel died, they stood still." (2 Samuel 2:23) No doubt they thought, "What a waste of a fine young life."

Eventually the Lord showed me why He had directed my focus to this story.

Asahel is a perfect model of the immature believer. He has great strengths and abilities and knows what they are. He uses them well. He has potential. The problem is that, like most youths, he also has glaring weaknesses but no clue as to what they are. So, he goes out to take on a champion, planning to use his strengths and abilities, but gets defeated by his weakness.

Eventually, thinking about Asahel situation, a principle **for reaching one's full potential** or a formula for achieving success—whatever we wish to call it—began to formulate itself. It looks like this:

I know my strengths and I know my weaknesses. I use my strengths and I guard against my weaknesses.

Everyone is a combination of strengths and weaknesses. The trick is to know what they are and to use the strength without letting the weakness trip us up.

What were Asahel's strengths? He was young, athletic, a runner. He had a great heritage, with David as his uncle. He was daring, perhaps a man of faith.

However.

He had numerous weaknesses. He was inexperienced in battle and exercised poor judgement. Abner gave him great counsel--"Better get yourself some armor, boy!"-- but like many a passionate youth, he could not take advice. He had no armor and apparently no weapon.

So--

Did Asahel use his strengths? He did.

Did he guard against his weaknesses? He did not.

Had we asked, I expect Asahel would have replied that he had no weaknesses. None that he knew of. Which was his problem, of course.

The question then becomes: *How does this formula apply to all of life or to other characters and teachings of Scripture? Or does it?*

It does indeed. In fact, it fits beautifully with quite a number of characters and stories in the Bible.

Consider the examples of these Bible characters....

David was facing Goliath. (I Samuel 17) David walked out into the Valley of Elah that day, fully aware of his strengths: his faith, his skill with a sling, his experience facing lions and bears; and also of his weaknesses: his size (so he would not be wearing King's Saul's armor which was several sizes too large!) and his inexperience in hand-to-hand combat with giants.

David used those strengths: he took out his sling and began selecting stones to fling at the Philistine giant.

But he guarded against his weaknesses: he refused Saul's armor, and stayed way back out of reach of Goliath.

By wisely using his strengths and guarding against his weaknesses, David won a great victory.

On the other hand, there is Mephibosheth, the son of David's best friend Jonathan (II Samuel 9).

This sad young man had strengths of which he was unaware and thus did not use them, and weaknesses that he knew full well, which were keeping him immobilized.

Mephibosheth was the last of the lineage of King Saul and thus—to his mind at least—a wanted man. He was lame in both feet, the result of a childhood accident (II Samuel 4:4). He lived outside the country in constant fear.

What he did not know was that his father Jonathan had provided for him in a pact with David years earlier, that the survivor would care for the other's offspring. So, here is Mephibosheth with all kinds of good things in his favor, but he knows none of them. All he knows are the negatives in his situation.

So, following our formula: Mephibosheth does not know his strengths, so he does not use them. He knows only his weaknesses, and they are destroying him.

Finally, I wondered if Scripture shows us a man who knew neither his strengths nor his weaknesses. Such a person would be a stranger to himself, unaware of what he could do and should never try. It hit me: that's the Simon Peter of the Gospels.

Take Matthew 16. In this one chapter, Jesus compliments Peter for his spiritual discernment (vs. 17). That's his strength. Then, a few minutes later, Jesus rebukes Peter for being a dullard and even calls him Satan (vv. 22-23), meaning "adversary." His weakness.

However, Peter knew neither what his strengths were in Christ nor what his weaknesses of the flesh were. As a result, he was hot and cold, up one day and down the next.

The final result of all this looks something like this:

IMMATURITY: I know my strengths and use them; I do not know my weaknesses and thus do not guard against them. (Example: Asahel in II Samuel 2.)

INVINCIBILITY: I know my strengths and use them; I know my weaknesses and guard against them. (Example: David facing Goliath in I Samuel 17.)

INFERIORITY: I do not have a clue about my strengths, so do not use them; I could talk all day about my weaknesses—I have so many—but do not guard against them. (Example: Mephibosheth in II Samuel 7.)

INCONSISTENCY: I do not know my strengths and I do not know my weaknesses. Sometimes I stumble upon my strengths and use them, but sometimes not; sometimes I guard against my weaknesses and sometimes not. (Example: Simon Peter in Matthew 16.)

Okay...

At this point, all this is, is a nice Bible study. So it has to be applied to everyday life. How does this apply to your personal life or to the lives of public figures in the news? How would it apply to those teenagers you work with in your church? the deacons? parents?

And how does the Lord want you to use what He has shown to be true?

Before leaving this, let's point out that Goliath himself is a wonderful case study in this formula. He had great positives: size, brute strength, experience in battle, massive weapons, a shield-bearer running in front of him, and armor to envelope his huge body. However, he has one glaring weakness which David has spotted: in order to see out his helmet, he has left an opening. And that opening is just the right size for one of

David's stones. David bends over and finds stones just the size to fit inside that eyehole and that's where he aims.

When the Apostle Peter said Satan roams to and fro like a roaring lion, seeking whom he may devour (I Peter 5:8), it takes no great imagination to figure that he is looking for our weaknesses so he can focus his attack there.

That's how it's done, pastor. At least, that's how I do it with a great deal of help from the Lord. You'll have your own way. The Holy Spirit is wonderful about doing something different in each individual. That's part of the fun of working with Him.

There is no one else like you. And thus, no one else is going to have the Scriptural insights as you. The Holy Spirit will do an original work in you. Count on it.

Trust Him.

Now, think about the part of the ministry that is bothering you the most, the scripture story that has captured your heart, the aspect of the Lord's work you have the most trouble with or fun doing. See if the Lord is up to something.

CHAPTER THREE

When the Preacher is a Joke--and How to Prevent that from Happening

It sounded cruel, but he was not a believer and his assessment of the former pastor was an honest statement of how he felt.

After staying with a church of their denomination for too long–watching the pastor drive people away by his lack of ministry, his poor leadership, and a neglect of everything that makes a church authentic–the entire family reluctantly moved their membership to a church a few miles away. What they found there was striking in its contrast.

The congregation was warm and friendly, the church was thriving, and the pastoral team was outstanding. The minister's sermons were powerful, biblical, and convicting. When a grandchild went into the hospital for surgery, this pastor left home before 5 am and met the family in the medical center. After praying with them, he stayed until the medical staff reported that the surgery had ended, and the child was doing great.

After he left, the son-in-law, father of the child who had just come through surgery, offered his assessment of the contrast between this new pastor and the old one who was still in the former church. "The other one was a joke," he said.

A joke.

The family member who reported this to me observed, "We would not agree with Bobby that any minister is a joke. Remember, Bobby is unsaved and was not raised in the church. This is his honest reaction." Then she said, "But we cannot help but be struck with the contrast in the sermons of the two men."

"How were they different?" I asked.

"The former minister filled his sermon time with jokes and funny stories, then ended with a short devotional thought. The new minister preaches a powerful message direct from God's Word, the kind of sermon that cuts and convicts and inspires and blesses."

The contrast between those two preachers and their sermons deserves closer analysis. Let's give it a try.

The Pastor is a Joke.

That brutal assessment stings, I admit. Having preached hundreds of sermons–thousands, probably–over nearly 60 years, no doubt I have delivered many that could have been described as several funny stories ending with a devotional thought.

I say that to my shame.

In defense of the "former" pastor, the one who earned this put-down from Bobby, I imagine he preaches the way he learned. Perhaps he did not have a good role model after which to pattern himself.

That's no excuse, of course. Unless the pastor has lived under a rock or in a vacuum, he surely has heard others preach. Thanks to the internet, any of us can find a thousand sermons at our fingertips which we can hear seated at our desk.

So, my defense of him will not hold.

One wonders whether this "former" pastor is paying attention to the signs all around him that his ministry is not working out. And what are those signs? Surely, he has noticed the severely diminishing attendance, key leaders leaving for other churches, finances dropping through the basement, and several of the finest Christian people he knows informing him earnestly and humbly why they can no longer abide his ministry.

From all reports, that church is on life support at the moment.

What if that pastor had had a strong friend speak sternly to him years ago?

Faithful are the wounds of a friend; but deceitful are the kisses of an enemy. (Proverbs 27:6)

We have no clue whether or not anyone tried. But someone should have tried to tell him that he was undermining his ministry, abandoning God's people, and forsaking the call of God on his life.

No pastor should be a jokester in the pulpit.

When Lot, Abraham's nephew, began to warn his family members to flee because of the coming judgment of God upon Sodom, no one took him seriously. *To his sons-in-law he seemed to be joking.* (Genesis 19:14)

I wonder about that. Was Lot a jokester, always kidding? Did he pull pranks and play practical jokes?

Those of us who love a great story or a funny tale and often drop a great joke into our sermons should take caution. If we do it much, we lose our spiritual authority with the congregation. We come across as an entertainer, not as God's man with His message.

In time, like Lot's sons-in-law, people will have a hard time telling when we are kidding and when we are dead serious.

There is hardly a worse indictment on a man's preaching than that.

In order to earn and maintain his moral authority with the congregation, a pastor must intentionally set out to do certain things:

1. He must be a man of prayer.

To make a difference personally and through his preaching, the living God must permeate the pastor and anoint his sermons. It's that simple: Pray or fail. (Luke 18:1)

2. He must be a man of the Word.

Unless he devotes himself to filling his mind with Scripture and constantly working to understand its meaning and apply it in his world, his sermons will be "I think" and "I believe" and "something I read in the paper the other day." He will tell the jokes he heard and place his own thoughts on an equal level with Scripture. The sermons will become shallow and ineffective, the congregation bored out of their minds, with no one being convicted or challenged or converted. When that happens, Satan's horde quietly dismisses such a preacher as a force to be reckoned with.

3. He must minister to the people during the week if he expects them to hear him on Sunday.

George W. Truett used to say he diagnosed in the homes during the week so he could prescribe from the pulpit on Sunday. Without a personal ministry that involves meeting individuals in need *in some way* during the week, his sermons will have little relevance to anything anyone is dealing with.

4. He must value the time he spends in the pulpit as the most important hour of the week.

By treasuring this time when he represents the living God before his people, a minister will study the craft of preaching and devote himself to learning how to do it better and better. No one ever learns it all, but if he keeps at it, he will find how he personally works best, studies best, and preaches most effectively.

Many a pastor would be surprised to know that the congregation can tell the difference when he is prayed up and studied up and when he cut corners that week in his preparation. For me personally, I can tell it by whether the bucket I'm drawing from is almost empty or running over. The congregation can tell it by the ease with which the ideas flow, the aptness of each Scripture verse I share, and the power with which they hit home.

Recently, I was surfing the net looking for what preachers had written on a particular subject when I ran across a minister's website in which I could listen to his sermons. I selected one, clicked the appropriate places, and sat back in my office chair to listen.

Fifteen minutes into the sermon, I clicked it off. That minister had told joke after joke for 10 minutes, then launched into a pre-sermon prayer that seemed to be without direction or an end. By the time the sermon should have been half over, he had not started yet.

I do not know that man and so have no opportunity to say this to him publicly, nor do I wish to. But I find myself wishing Bobby would sit in his congregation long enough to tell him something I don't have the nerve to say: Preacher, you are a joke.

Some things, even a lost man knows.

CHAPTER FOUR

Fear Has No Place in The Ministry

Fear is a constant companion with many a minister.

The problem is most do not recognize it as fear. The monster takes many disguises and can even show up as our closest friend.

The pastor who refuses to preach on a touchy subject because someone in his congregation is engaged in it is not acting from compassion or discretion. It's good old-fashioned fear.

The pastor who refuses to train his people in faithful stewardship principles or shrinks from preaching on money because he hates being accused of money-grabbing is motivated, not by wise caution but by fear.

The pastor who will not stand up to a deacon bully, who cow-tows to a matron who controls everyone, who keeps catering to unreasonable demands from the congregation because he does not like to "cause waves," that pastor is living in fear and undermining his own ministry.

Nothing about fear pleases God. No ministry that finds its source in fear of people is of God. No powerful sermon, no sacrificial gift, no pastoral ministry, no church program rooted in fear of someone or some group has the blessings of Heaven.

Fear hath torment, according to I John 4:18.

We all know what fear feels like. You were middle-aged before taking your first plane ride. You took your grandchildren on that death-defying ride at Six Flags. You were giving a memorized speech to the entire student body and forgot the last half. You were playing a piano recital or performing in a school play and at a critical moment lost your way and died in front of everyone.

It's no fun humiliating yourself. Thereafter, the fear of doing just that can control your life if you're not careful.

Why did you fear? Where is your faith? (Mark 4:40)

We have to choose. Faith and fear are sworn enemies. They cannot co-exist inside the Lord's disciples.

If faith is confidence in Jesus, fear is the absence of it.

Again and again in the Gospels, we read that certain ones "feared the people." That is quite an indictment upon leaders who should have been out front setting the example, blazing the path. Instead, with timid souls and cowardly hearts, they took their own version of polls–public opinion sampling is as old as humanity–to see what they could safely do without offending their constituents.

King Herod would have executed John, but "he feared the crowd since they regarded him as a prophet" (Matthew 14:5). Later, he executed John anyway because as much as he feared the people, he feared his wife's displeasure even more.

The religious leaders refused to answer Jesus honestly because "we're afraid of the crowd" (Matthew 21:26).

No one in Jerusalem was speaking openly of Jesus because "they feared the Jews," a reference to the religious leaders (John 7:13).

Joseph of Arimathea was a disciple of Jesus, we read, but "secretly because of his fear of the Jews" (John 19:38).

On the first Easter afternoon, the disciples are gathered behind locked doors "because of their fear of the Jews" (John 20:19).

So much fear.

Fear intimidates us into doing the wrong thing, or more likely, doing nothing.

It's a human thing. We do not like to stand apart from the accepted custom, to be exposed, to have everyone looking at us, particularly if in anger.

Often, we who are called leaders should more appropriately be termed "people-pleasers."

So, we stay back with the crowd and do the safe thing.

God is not pleased. Not in the least.

To youthful Jeremiah, God said: *Do not be afraid of anyone, for I am with you to deliver you.* And again: *Stand up and tell them everything that I command you. Do not be intimidated by them or I will cause you to cower before them.*

Easy for the Lord to say, right? But wait. God proceeded to make Jeremiah a fascinating promise:

Today, I have made you a fortified city, an iron pillar, and bronze walls against the whole land—against the kings of Judah, its officials, its priests, and the population. They will fight against you but never prevail over you, since I am with you to rescue you. (Jeremiah 1)

The one that fascinates me is the *bronze wall*. Even though I've never seen one, I know what would happen when someone threw a rock (or a tomato) at it: it would bounce off.

God was promising to make Jeremiah impervious to personal attacks. Good thing, because he sure received his share and more during his long ministry.

Over a span of 42 years, I pastored six churches. The first I served for 14 months; the last three for a total of 30 years. I know what it is to lead a church and serve the Lord from fear. From time to time, it was a personal thing for me and at other times, I recognized it in fellow pastors.

Fear does a lot of things to a pastor, none of them good. Because of fear, a pastor will tiptoe around certain members. He will neglect his family in order to run to their beckoning. He will worry about his job, cut corners on areas of ministry, and will shape his sermons and even his daily living to suit his captors.

His captors. Did you get that?

Such a minister is not free. He is the captive of those who are calling the shots in his life.

It was for freedom that Christ has set us free. (Galatians 5:1)

This is one of those ironies or paradoxes of which the Christian life has an abundance. We are slaves to Christ, and we are free in Christ. We are servants of God's people, but we are free from all men (I Corinthians 9:19).

So, let us go serve all the people. But let us do it for Jesus' sake. (II Corinthians 4:5)

Let us not write our own emancipation proclamation. That was written for us at Calvary. Instead, let us find the freedom in Christ which He bought and paid for at that time.

God has not given us the spirit of fear, but of power and of love and of a sound mind. (II Timothy 1:7)

Not a fear of the devil and his forces, but power.

Not a fear of people, but love.

Not a fear of the unknown, but a sound mind.

Heavenly Father, deliver us from a fear of the forces of darkness and replace it with power, from a fear of the powers that be in our churches or denomination and replace it with love, and from a fear of the unknown—whether it brings prosperity or economic disaster, health or sickness, life or death—and replace it with soundness of mind.

Empower us with thy Spirit with the kind of boldness that comes from fearing the displeasure of Thee alone and no one else. Through Christ our Lord, Amen.

CHAPTER FIVE

"My Pastor's Not Always Right, But He's Never in Doubt."

The pastor who is never in doubt, no matter whether he's right or wrong, is part of the problem. In fact, he is a huge problem.

Such a minister will attract a certain kind of church member, the kind that likes pure certainties with no grey areas and nothing left undecided. This church member prefers someone else do his thinking for him. When asked what he believes or why he believes a particular doctrine, he replies, "See my pastor."

What the know-for-certainty-in-all-areas pastor does, however, is to drive away anyone with a critical faculty, the kind who thinks matters through and asks uncomfortable questions. Luke found such Christians in Berea, who *examined the Scriptures daily to see if these things were so.* (Acts 17:11)

Let's address this tendency in some of us preachers to be the court of last resort, the final word on all things theological, for our people.

Woe to you experts in the law! You have taken away the key of knowledge! You didn't go in yourselves, and you hindered those who were going in! (Luke 11:52)

The scribes started out as copyists of the Word when it was hand-written on parchment or skins and costly to possess. The scribes filled a helpful role and provided a needed service. In time, however, they ended up as self-appointed experts whose word people accepted as law.

Not good.

I'm tempted to say, "Beware when anyone calls you an expert on anything." But worse than that–and this is our focus here–is when you think of yourself as an expert. That was where the scribes had landed the day Jesus castigated them.

When we start thinking of ourselves as an expert on any matter that concerns ministry, a number of things happen. None of them good.

When you start believing yourself an expert on God things….

1) You begin to pontificate. You become insufferable.

2) You cannot bear for someone to disagree with you. You become intolerant of dissension.

3) Pride becomes your chief adornment.

4) You close yourself to new insights, further revelation, and people with helpful input.

5) You begin to shrivel inside.

6)) You set yourself up as a judge on all who believe otherwise.

7) You become a challenge for a lot of people. They ache to see you humbled. You might as well draw a target on your back, for from that moment on, you are in their crosshairs.

Somewhere I read that President Franklin D. Roosevelt had an innate distrust of experts. That's not a bad thing to have when you're trying to lead a nation out of a depression and through a world war and are surrounded by a mob telling you how to do your job. I think it's fair to say from reading history that there were few, if any, genuine experts in either economics or military matters in those days or ours. There are people with experience or book learning or philosophies or ideas and theories, and who think this sets them apart from the masses.

Various television meteorologists with Ph.D. after their names are introduced as the resident "hurricane expert" or "tornado expert" or "disaster expert." Anyone who thinks there are experts in weather-forecasting has not been paying attention.

Preachers fall into this trap.

A preacher who loves to study his Bible and dedicates himself to learning the biblical languages is all set to do some serious work in the Word. Nothing wrong and everything right with that.

The danger comes when he lights in on some pet theory or favorite theologian or event in theological history and goes to seed on it. In time, he may actually know more than almost anyone. At this point, he's walking on his "high place."

High place?

That's what it's called in Habakkuk 3:19 and Psalm 18:33. Think of that as scaling Everest. Finally you arrive at the peak. The view is magnificent, the feeling is breath-taking, and the sense of accomplishment is inspiring. However, the air is thin, your head gets dizzy and the footing becomes slippery.

Be careful on your high places, preacher. You could get in big trouble up here.

Treat this as simply a call for checking your humility and childlikeness from time to time. When you have done it all–gotten those terminal degrees, written those books, spoken from those public forums, and received all those awards–say to yourself, "I am an unworthy servant; I have only done my duty." (Luke 17:10)

Back to the scribes for a moment or two.

You have taken away the key of knowledge. You did not enter in yourselves and those who were entering in, you hindered.

1) They had the key of knowledge.

The point here is that **knowledge was the key.** Before one can be saved, he/she needs to know how. And how shall they know unless someone tells them, as Paul said in Romans 10.

The student of the Word learns how to be saved and to live for God. He reads and sees and knows what Christ said and presumably, knows what it means. He has the key of knowledge.

A key is a powerful thing. With it, you can open lots of doors.

2) They refused to enter.

Learning was more important to the scribes than actually doing. Intellectual delights had become their meat and potatoes, as the saying goes. The Lord Jesus said, *if you know these things, blessed are you if you do them.* (John 13:17)

In C. S. Lewis' "The Great Divorce," we have a fantasy about a busload of people in hell being allowed to visit Heaven and then decide whether they wanted to remain. (Lewis' contention is that they would be so out of place in Heaven, they would be miserable.) Anyway, one of the priests in perdition asked a Heavenly resident whether intellectual inquiries were welcomed in the land of God. After all, he said, he was set to deliver a paper in hell next week on the search for the historical Jesus. Or some such.

"Is there intellectual freedom?" he asked. The answer was, "No. Only God."

The question is whether He is enough.

3) They hindered those trying to get in.

The scribes rejected both John the Baptist and Jesus. By their teaching, they emphasized the petty demands of the law and laid them without pity on the poor souls coming to them for counsel.

Two residents of Jericho came to Jesus over the hindrances of the people about them. At the end of Luke 18, it was blind Bartimaeus who ignored the crowd's discouragement in order to get to Jesus. A few verses later, in Luke 19, it was Zacchaeus who was unable to see the Lord because of the crowd blocking the view.

Once in the late 1970s, Yazoo City's Jerry Clower, the celebrated Christian entertainer and godly Baptist deacon, told the state Baptist convention in Jackson about an integrated choir from the local Baptist college being invited for a concert in his church. Once some people heard that the choir contained an African American or two, they went ballistic. So, in the time-honored way by which we Baptists resolve our differences (to the extent we can!), a church-wide business meeting was held.

What struck my friend Jerry about that was that people whose names were on the church rolls but *who never came to church,* showed up to vote against the choir concert. He said, "Think of it. They don't come to church themselves. And the only time they show up is to vote to keep someone else from coming."

Hypocrites.

Jesus called the scribes and their cohorts, the Pharisees, hypocrites. They were the opposite of what they seemed to be.

Hypocrisy is ugly in everyone except us. We see politicians preaching frugality in government and voting themselves extra benefits. We see leaders building careers on patriotic issues and family values, then being revealed to have sold their souls for an hour of pleasure or a few dollars.

With ourselves, however, hypocrisy shows up not as the ugly monster it appeared in the politician, but as a friend. Our own hypocrisies are simply our attempts to deal with our weakness of the flesh, our need for security for our family, our desire to be re-elected so we can go on acting in the public interest.

One writer says the scribes of the First Century turned God's Word into a book of riddles and puzzles which only they could interpret. Caught up in a religion of their own making, they no longer had anything to offer a seeking, hurting soul.

They had shut the door of God's mercy and grace and thrown away the key.

One of the most endearing qualities of a spiritual leader is the humble realization that he too is an unworthy sinner in desperate need of a daily outpouring of God's grace; the constant awareness that if he got what he deserved, he would be in hell; and that when he stands to preach God's mercy and grace, no one is needier than himself.

Once he quits believing this, he becomes part of the problem and no longer an aspect of the answer.

"Humble yourself under the mighty hand of God" was written not just for the pagan outsider, but for the righteous believer also.

CHAPTER SIX

The Pastor's Comeuppance

My friend David told me what happened.

Dave was pastoring a small church in a southern town while living in a nearby city. During the week, he worked at the health department.

One day, his church leadership requested that Dave get ordained. He passed this on to his home church pastor in the city.

The pastor said, "Dave, anyone in particular you want to preach your ordination?" Dave couldn't think of anyone. "I'll leave that to you," he said.

The night of the big event, Dave entered the church sanctuary and spotted a colleague from the health department. As they exchanged greetings, the friend said, "Uh, Dave. Have you seen who's preaching your service tonight?" He hadn't.

As soon as he laid eyes on the featured preacher, Dave stood there in shock.

That preacher was a retired pastor who lived in the city. Only a few weeks before, Dave had served him with official papers demanding that he take care of some health issues on his property or face legal action. The preacher had defiantly cursed David out, creating quite a spectacle.

"He did take the remedial action we demanded, however," Dave says.

But even so.

The preacher who cursed David out is now about to preach his ordination service.

No doubt the old preacher had not had a clue who this young pastor was. He had accepted the city pastor's invitation blindly.

And now he was facing a little version of his own personal Judgement Day.

The old pastor was receiving a comeuppance.

Just before the service got underway, the older man sidled over to Dave and whispered, "I think we can just forget about that little incident between us the other day, don't you?"

And because Pastor Dave is the gentleman the old man should have been but wasn't, he agreed.

One wonders what would happen if every pastor's audience next Sunday was composed exclusively of men and women with whom he has had dealings in the last year.

We enter the sanctuary from the organ side.

Over here on the left sits the mechanic who worked on the pastor's wife's car. Down the pew is the waitress at his favorite coffee shop with her family. Behind them we notice the grocery store checker along with two teenage girls who fill in for her from time to time. They all wonder if the preacher is as impatient to move the service along in his church as he is when they're waiting on him.

The pastor's barber is there, right beside his plumber and his electrician. The trashmen are here too. Fortunately, they are wearing their good clothes today. Behind them sits the newspaper delivery person. They've all heard enough complaints from the pastor about lousy service to stoke their curiosity about the kind of sermon such a preacher would deliver.

Sitting halfway back is a group the pastor doesn't recognize. These are the telephone service people from his local department store, the internet provider, the phone company, and Amazon. Some speak broken English, but enough to get by. The pastor was more than a little impatient with all of these on the phone recently.

The children's schoolteachers are here, along with the assistant principal. The college where the pastor's son attends is represented by the campus minister and the woman who works in the business office. The pastor had words with her a few days ago.

The pastor rises to begin the service. He strides to the center of the platform and glances out at his audience. Hesitating, now for the first time in weeks, he transforms his usual invocation into a genuine Lord-help-me prayer.

Assuming the pastor to be a man of genuine integrity with a heart for God and people, the experience of seeing before him a large group of people who have had contact with him in some of his less flattering moments would be a great thing.

Granted, we are assuming a lot. The pastor who is rude to service people and who throws his weight around with "lesser mortals" cannot be assumed to value integrity or have a heart for God. If such rudeness is a pattern for him, then he is what may be officially termed a hypocrite. And that makes him an embarrassment to the cause of Christ.

If he has little or no integrity and less a heart for God and people than for his own power and position, then he will bull his way through the worship service today with scarcely a thought about the people he has trampled upon who would love to see some humility from him today.

But if his rudeness was the exception, then he looks upon the congregation today as an opportunity to right some wrongs. His leadership today will involve a number of powerful influences.

He will be humble. Above all, he feels a sense of his own sinful heart and his constant need of grace, both from God and from others.

He will be specific. The old pastor who leaned over to my friend Dave asked if they could put "that little incident" behind them. That's not good enough. That was the equivalent of sweeping it under the rug and asking the victim to okay the act. There needs to be a specific confession for what he has done.

He will be apologetic. He will ask for forgiveness. And he will extend forgiveness and mercy to anyone needing it from him.

He will be Christlike. He need not grovel or humiliate himself. He would be receiving forgiveness and possibly extending it, receiving love and giving it.

He will seize the moment for a lesson from God's word. The choices of stories from Scripture are almost endless.

But since we are fantasizing here, it's probably as far as we need to journey in this direction.

The minister's conduct is never a private matter. He is no private citizen but a servant of God on mission in an alien land. He is an ambassador for Jesus Christ. People are making decisions about Jesus and eternity based on what they see in him.

Is that unfair? Whether it is or not, the pastor should have known this goes with the territory when he accepted the call into the ministry. It's who you are.

His situation is not unlike an American soldier stationed in a foreign country. He wears his uniform into the city and engage people in conversation and various dealings as he buys items, eats in restaurants, takes in a movie. The people however do not see him as the individual that he is. They see an American soldier. They make decisions about Americans and our military based on his conduct.

Imagine the U.S. Ambassador to Britain (officially, "The Court of St. James") saying to the President who appointed him, "I can't imagine you asking me to do that thing. I have my rights, you know. Why should I act any differently in London than anyone else?" The president sighs and says, "May I remind you, Ambassador, you are there by my appointment. I can recall you any time I please. Your entire purpose in that country is to do my bidding. What part of that don't you understand?"

And so, the Christian in this world–but particularly the minister of the Lord Jesus Christ–may put up with a great deal of hassle and misbehavior without retaliating. He knows that he is representing the Lord Jesus and that people will draw conclusions about his Savior by what he does. Sometimes he might even resent that, but this is the life he signed on for.

After all....

The driver the pastor just cut off in traffic turns out to be his next appointment. So, he will "drive unto others as he would have them drive unto him."

The father of the student the pastor chewed out for what he perceived to be mistreatment of his child turns out to be an important official he was about to ask for a favor. And so he will look for wise ways to stand up for his child when necessary.

No one is suggesting the preacher become a door mat.

We do suggest he become more like Jesus.

That doesn't seem like too much to ask.

Whatever you do, work at it with all your heart, as working for the Lord, not for men, since you know that you will receive an inheritance from the Lord as a reward. It is the Lord Christ you are serving. (Colossians 3:23-24)

** ** ** ** **

An afterthought....

Years ago, when I was the new pastor at the First Baptist Church of Columbus, Mississippi, they had a designated parking space for the pastor in the rear of the building. Since I visited the two local hospitals first thing every morning, often I would arrive to find my spot had been claimed by someone else. One morning, I decided to see who the culprit was.

I pulled my car up to the back bumper of the offending vehicle and went inside.

A few minutes later, a distraught young mother came into my office, all apologies. "Oh, Dr. McKeever, I am so sorry I got your space. It was raining and I had my hands full of diaper bags and papers and my baby was crying."

I felt like going through the floor.

That day, our custodian transformed that parking space into a "loading zone." And we painted over the names/titles of every staffer who had a designated space. We would not make this mistake again.

There will be no prima donnas on this church staff. We are here to serve.

CHAPTER SEVEN

The Apostle Paul's Gift to Preachers

I was with you in weakness, in fear, and in much trembling. (I Corinthians 2:3)

For reasons I cannot explain, this line from the great apostle has lodged itself in my heart over the past few days. The more I reflect on it, the more I appreciate Paul's admitting it.

In this and every other case where Paul mentions some kind of physical infirmity, we wish we had more information. Was he sick? Ailing? Still healing from previous beatings.

John MacArthur writes: *Paul came to Corinth after being beaten and imprisoned in Philippi, run out of Thessalonica and Berea, and scoffed at in Athens, so he may have been physically weak. But in that weakness, he was most powerful. There were no theatrics or techniques to manipulate people's response. His fear and shaking was because of the seriousness of his mission.* (The MacArthur Study Bible)

I suppose we preachers are a lot like horses and mules and dogs: hit us often enough and we become "gun shy." We want to stand and deliver with boldness and power, but we're ready to duck.

Thank you, Paul, for telling us this. And if you will allow me, I will draw a few inferences from it that I find helpful to all of us who stand to proclaim God's Word.

1. We appreciate the transparency, Paul.

It pleases me when a person we acknowledge to be "great" is not impressed by their own PR but continues to act like a real person. Paul had not read his own press clippings and so did not try to maintain a "public persona."

"This is what was going on inside me when I preached the Lord's message to you," the Apostle tells the Corinthian believers.

We have no idea what they made of that. Could be some scoffed at it. After all, we know from this and the Second Corinthian Epistle that some in that church were dismissing Paul as a first-class letter-writer but a Johnny-come-lately and a second-rate preacher and thus unworthy of the mantle of an apostle.

What I make of his statement, however, is this: he's the real deal.

And don't we appreciate that about him.

2. We too often proclaim the Gospel in weakness.

All over the world, God's preachers are mistreated and harassed and persecuted. Just because we in America aren't, for the most part, should not make us miss this point. Many stand in pulpits (or in jails or on street corners) and through great pain and at great peril, proclaim the message of Jesus Christ and His redemption.

The weakness pastors in this country endure while delivering the Word of the Lord tends to be of another type. I have stood to lead worship services and deliver the Lord's message when sitting in the pews staring me down were some who despised me and were doing all in their power to get me fired. The preacher quickly learns to put his eyes on the Lord and look only to Him for affirmation.

My brother Ron has preached almost all his adult life as a diabetic, with the limitations that disease imposes and the regimen it requires.

Other pastors and preachers deal with other kinds of infirmities. God bless them. They read this statement from Paul and know the feeling.

3. We appreciate hearing what the great apostle had to contend with.

For reasons I cannot fully understand or adequately explain, when we learn that others who went before us in this work endured great hardship *of the same type, we daily deal with* it helps. It's not anything as shallow as "misery loves company." It's more like, "This apparently is the norm. If they had to deal with this kind of trouble, it does not have to mean I'm failing in some way."

That's why the ordeals of Moses in leading Israel through Sinai's wilderness are instructive and oddly affirming to us. Time and again, we read how the people "murmured" against the man of God. Modern translations will change that to "grumbling," "were loud in their complaints," and such, but "murmuring" does it for me. The word carries the muffled background sounds of cowards who dare not confront their leader, but lurk around the edges of the crowd to infect them with their discontent.

Consider Him who endured such hostility from sinners against Himself, lest you become weary and discouraged in your souls. (Hebrews 12:3)

We gain strength and determination from watching how our Lord endured the persecutions and hostilities flung His way. In the same way, we are encouraged by seeing that God's lesser servants put up with the same treatment.

4. We see here a great lesson taught all through the Word.

That lesson is given eloquently in Paul's next epistle to these people. *Lest I should be exalted above measure by the abundance of the revelations, a thorn in the flesh was given to me.... And He said to me, "My grace is sufficient for you, for My strength is made perfect in weakness." Therefore most gladly I will rather boast in my infirmities, that the power of Christ may rest upon me.* (II Corinthians 12:7-10)

God loves to use small things, little gifts, and weak people. He delights in using congregations of a few people, people with little or no talents, and small acts of service. Why? *That no flesh should glory in His presence.* (I Corinthians 1:29)

5. No one enjoys being weak. However, it's no excuse for anything.

As John the Baptist saw himself fading into the background and Jesus of Nazareth rising to the forefront, he must have remembered his own words, spoken earlier before they carried the impact they did now. *He must increase; I must decrease.* (John 3:30)

When the Apostle Paul was berated as an unworthy impostor, accused of falsely claiming the credentials of a genuine apostle, he responded not as we would have expected. He could have shown his critics his educational accomplishments and rolled out the impressive list of his accomplishments and cited his stellar references. He did none of this. Instead, he spoke of his weaknesses.

From the Jews five times I received forty stripes minus one. Three times I was beaten with rods; once I was stoned; three times I was shipwrecked; a night and a day I have been in the deep; in journeys often, in perils of waters, in perils of robbers, in perils of my own countrymen, in perils of the Gentiles, in perils in the city, in perils in the wilderness, in perils in the sea, in perils among false brethren; in weariness and toil, in sleeplessness often, in hunger and thirst, in fastings often, in cold and nakedness…. (II Corinthians 11:24-27)

In the Tyndale Commentaries, Leon Morris quotes a second-century writing (*Acts of Paul and Thecla*) that purported to describe the physical appearance of the Apostle Paul:

A man of small stature, with a bald head and crooked legs, in a good state of body, with eyebrows meeting and nose somewhat crooked.

The Phillips translation of I Corinthians 2:3 has Paul saying: "I was feeling far from strong; I was nervous and rather shaky."

In his commentary on this epistle, Gordon Fee adds: "At the heart of (Paul's) preaching stood the 'weakness of God' (1:25), the story of a crucified Messiah (v.2). His own weakness served as a further visible demonstration of the same message, but even more to demonstrate that the message was of divine, not human, origin. Thus the apostle regularly glories in his weaknesses, not because he enjoyed ill health but because they were a sure evidence that the power was of God and not of himself."

Fee adds that Paul is "gladly willing that the Corinthians should now recall, so that they will be reminded of how unlike the Sophists (his critics) his preaching and appearance truly were."

I suggest we think of Paul's weaknesses, his trembling, his fearfulness while preaching in Corinth, as a gift to us.

–It reminds us that we have this treasure in earthen pots (II Corinthians 4:7). The point of that is "that the excellence of the power may be of God and not of us."

–It banishes forever our tendency to grab any excuse to get out of doing our duty. If he could do it, so can we.

If we had to wait until there were no obstacles to serve the Lord, nothing would ever get done. If we waited until all conditions were favorable, no one would ever set sail.

—It puts us in our place. We are only messengers, not the message.

In former days, when Western Union boys delivered printed communications to homes, no one rejected a message because the uniformed fellow at the door was found to be objectionable. He was irrelevant.

—In fact, it might even be good news. Perhaps, on the days when we feel especially poor, God might decide to do something extra special, just to show that He is in charge and can use the poorest of vessels.

Half a century ago, my friend Bill Nimmons served as assistant pastor of the great First Baptist Church of Starkville, Mississippi. Meanwhile, the pastor, Dr. D. C. Applegate, was dealing with a debilitating illness that eventually ended his life. Sometimes, Bill would get the call on Saturday night to be prepared to preach the next day. Once he got the call an hour before church on Sunday morning.

That day, his sermon was particularly effective. At the conclusion of the service, the chairman of deacons teasingly announced: "This morning, we saw what God can do. Now, come back for this evening's service and we will see what Bill can do."

Given a choice, we would all prefer seeing what God can do. If, in order for that to happen, His messenger must recede into the background and even carry a limitation of some kind, then so be it.

CHAPTER EIGHT

You Meet the Strangest People

Have you ever met a children's worker who hated kids? I have.

Have you ever seen a preacher who did not believe in God? My friend John Armistead attended some divinity school classes with such people at Berkeley.

Have you ever met a Bible teacher who did not believe the Bible? The woods are filled with them.

It takes all kinds, they say. I reckon so.

I thought of some of the weird people we meet in the ministry this week while reading Pat Conroy's book, *My Reading Life*. For everyone who loves to read, I cannot recommend this too highly. Every chapter is a delight. And for anyone who loves to write, ditto; every sentence is a wonder.

As a military brat, Conroy's family moved around a lot. When they settled in Beaufort, SC, he found it hard to form new friendships and while dodging the campus bullies discovered the school library. This became his favorite place. The odd thing, however, is that the librarian resented him coming in and reading books.

I thought you'd appreciate Conroy's tale about the librarian who hated readers. Here's the story....

Pastoring

Wandering through the stacks, young Pat Conroy came upon Victor Hugo's *Les Miserables*. So, he pulled it out, took a chair at a table, and delved into the world of Jean Valjean. For the next two weeks, he visited the library during off periods and read that book.

And then one day he met the librarian.

Her name was Eileen Hunter. "I had heard of Miss Hunter," Conroy writes. "She was famous among both teachers and students for her legendary temper and her need for absolute control of her book-lined fiefdom."

"When she spotted me reading Hugo she reacted as though I'd taken a box of Crayolas to the Book of Kells."

"What on earth are you doing here?" she said.

"I'm reading a book, ma'am," I said.

"I can see that. Do I look like an idiot or something? It's against the rules for a student to be in the library during lunchtime."

Then she said, "What's that book you're reading?"

She grabbed the volume from his hands and studied it like it were pornographic.

"She eyed me with a ferocious scowl. 'This book's never even been checked out. Are you reading it for the dirty parts?'"

Pat said, "I didn't know it had dirty parts."

"If it does," Miss Hunter said, "I'll toss it with the morning trash. If you find anything dirty report it directly to me. Hugo's a Frenchman. I don't like his books."

She suggested that Pat might prefer to read something Hugo had written about a football team. A book called *The Hunchback of Notre Dame*. I'm not making this up.

Conroy writes, "Checking a book out of the Beaufort High School library required a swashbuckling, adventurous spirit, as Miss Hunter patrolled those aisles with the austerity of a knight-errant. Whenever she checked out a book, she treated the poor student as she would a visiting pirate. For Miss Hunter I think that the state of nirvana would be a library cleaned of all readers and the books all shelved and accounted for. As a librarian, she was legendary in all the wrong ways and for all the wrong reasons."

There's a funny aspect to this sad little tale. After Conroy's graduation from The Citadel, he returned to Beaufort to teach for a while and dealt with Miss Hunter as a faculty member and a colleague.

"She was as cranky and adversarial as ever and would light into me with her complaints as I would bring four or five novels to check out for my weekly reading."

Pat's way of handling her was to tease her, to tell her that he knew she adored him and dreamed of him at night.

Then something unexpected happened.

Pastoring

One day he received a note from Miss Hunter asking him to meet her in the library after school. His curiosity was aroused.

"I don't know if you've noticed it lately, Conroy," she told him, "but I've come down with a summer cold."

The trouble, she went on to say, was that cold medicine did not work with her. The only thing that seemed to help was…. are you ready for this?….was a shot of bourbon.

Pat said, "So you want me to buy you a bottle of bourbon?"

She said, "A half-gallon of Jack Daniel's Black. There is a delivery box for Coburn Dairy beside my front door. Come after nightfall. Be discreet. There'll be an envelope with the exact amount of the purchase waiting for you. This is for medicinal purposes only. I've had trouble shaking this cold."

And how long had she been bothered by this problem?

"I've had this summer cold for about the last twenty years."

For the next two years Pat Conroy supplied the school librarian with her cold medicine, "always with discretion and under the cover of darkness."

She was lonely, Conroy writes. "In the years I knew her I never saw her reading a book or talking about a book she'd read."

At the end of that chapter, I scribbled, "This alone was worth the price of the book."

Got any Eileen Hunter clones in your acquaintance? Any in your church, pastor?

I've had a finance chairman who did not want anyone to spend money. Oh, and he resented my attempts to raise funds.

I've seen a missions president who did not want to do missions.

I have not seen a prayer chairman who was against praying but I'm confident some of them were not much in the way of prayer.

Worst of all, I know a preacher who sometimes struggles with his faith, who does not read His Bible as regularly as he ought, who can read two novels a week and enjoy a baseball game on television when he ought to be preparing his sermons. He's not very spiritual and the wonder is that he keeps his job.

I know that one best of all. That one is me.

I may be the strangest bird in any congregation I've pastored.

People thought when I was urging them to pray for their pastor that it was only as a formality. They had no idea how desperately I needed their intercessions.

After over a half century of pastoring and religious leadership, I'd like to report that my spiritual maturity has grown to the point that they can now drop back and pray for lesser mortals. But I'm in as dire need of the prayers of God's people as I've ever been. Little has changed.

I can't say that I find comfort in the line from the Apostle Paul, but I sure understand it. *O wretched man that I am! Who will deliver me from this body of death?* (Romans 7:24)

Aren't we all thankful for the grace and mercy of God upon strange people like you and me?

I'm remembering something Pastor Bill Day told a group of us preachers who were meeting in his sanctuary one Monday morning. "There is a fellow who gives me a great deal of trouble. When I pastored in Florida, he was there, undermining everything I did by his criticism, his doubts, and his meanness. He kept hounding me, wanting to know if I really believed this, why had I not done a better job of preparing, that sort of thing. And worst of all, when I moved from Florida to this city, he came too. He's always there to remind me of my sins, my failures, and my weakness."

He paused and said, "It's me. I'm my own worst enemy."

Whatever else that does, it should make us more understanding of those in our congregation who do much the same thing.

CHAPTER NINE

What to Do When A Sermon Is Even Boring the Preacher

A pastor friend was telling some of us the sermon he is working on for next Sunday. The challenge, he said, was that part of the text is very difficult. "How to convey its message without getting too theological is my problem."

My own skeptical nature translated that as: "How to preach it without boring my people to death is what I'm up against!"

A day or two later, on my website we raised the question of what a pastor is to do when his guest preacher is boring the congregation. Most of us have been there/done that.

But there is a more urgent question....

What should the preacher do when it's his own preaching that is boring the people to tears?

Now, if he discovers that in the middle of a sermon, there's little he can do other than to shoot up an emergency prayer-flare for divine help or just cut his losses, end the sermon, and send the people home.

But if he is still in his study, he should know early on if this sermon is likely to bore his people. He can then decide to do whatever is necessary to make it listenable to them.

Question: *How does a pastor know on Tuesday that next Sunday's sermon will be boring?*

Here are some ways he can know for sure that this sermon is not going to connect with the people in the pew:

—the very subject is boring to him.

—he is unclear about the message he wishes to convey.

—the sermon is long on exegesis and short on application or relevance.

—he's getting into doctrinal areas he has not worked out in his own mind.

—the word "Jebusites" can be found anywhere in the body of the message.

Okay, I just dropped that last one in as a little tribute to Harry Emerson Fosdick. He famously said once that "no one comes to church on Sunday wondering what ever happened to the Jebusites." Indeed. (The ironic thing about this is that some of us love the details of biblical history to the point that we would welcome such a sermon! All the more reason to remind ourselves that few in the pews share this affliction.)

So, the pastor has decided on Tuesday that next Sunday's sermon has all the potential for putting Sleep-Eze out of business. What is he to do?

Here are some remedies we strongly recommend....

1) Stop all preparation on this message and drop to your knees. *It's prayer time!* *"Father, show me what to do!"*

An evangelist friend commented on my blog as to why so many hard-fought, strongly-believed and well-studied sermons are dead on delivery. "A lack of prayer," he said. "The Holy Spirit is the One who breathes life into a message. And He works by prayer."

So, let us ask Him what He wants to do about His message.

2) After praying, take a walk around the block. *Talk this sermon out to yourself. What is it about this subject that captivates you? Try verbalizing it.*

That, incidentally, is also the best sermon preparation I ever do. When the sermon is well into development, I take a long walk on the levee beside the Mississippi River and talk the message out. I actually speak it out, although not very loud. I usually carry a sheet of paper folded over several times and a pen. Preaching the sermon will suggest additional thoughts and insights and maybe a detour or two to avoid. Unless I jot them down on the spot, those flashes will have vanished by the time I return to the study.

3) Figure out what the primary thrust of this sermon should be and cut out all the stuff that does not

advance your theme. Stay with your original purpose, the one the Holy Spirit used to bring you to this subject in the first place.

I know what happens in the study. You are driven to a text by a burning desire to make a point the Lord has laid on your heart. But as you study and dig, you keep unearthing more and more good insights and inspiring points to make. Pretty soon, the original thought that brought you here is buried under a ton of great insights. When that happens, it's time to stop and dig out the Lord's message and shine it off and get back on course. *Stay with the plan.*

4) If the sermon still isn't coming together, call a friend. *Every pastor should have at least one older minister whom you can call on in a moment's notice.*

By this point your sermon needs the objective assessment and suggestions on how to make it work from an outsider, one who knows you, loves you and sympathizes with what you are trying to do here. You need a mentor.

5) Now, if it still isn't working, it's time to lay this sermon aside for the time being. *Next Sunday may not be the right time for this sermon. It may need to marinate.*

6) Eventually, if you cannot find the key to unlocking the heart of this message and making it work as a sermon, it's the better part of wisdom to walk away from it until the Lord opens it up for you. *You will know when He has pulled it from the recesses of your mind and heart and put it on the front burner once again.* (Hey, I can mix metaphors with the best of them!)

In response to the earlier message, where I was suggesting what a pastor could do when his guest preacher was boring the congregation, a friend known only from the internet challenged me. "What command of the Lord does this violate?" he wanted to know. "Perhaps the Lord told that preacher to say these things."

Good question. And it deserves a good response. The best one I know is found in John 21. Three times the Lord told the Apostle Peter to "feed my sheep."

The boring sermon—the one that misses the people, that dulls their minds and lulls them to sleep—is likely closer to straw than it is to grain. Jeremiah 23:28 comes to mind: *What does straw have in common with grain?*

Even the best preachers will sometimes fail to live up to his own high standards. Think of your favorite preacher. I guarantee that his people will tell you sometimes he hits it out of the park and sometimes he strikes out. No one is at his best all the time.

Two things about that need to be said....

One. Give yourself room to fail occasionally. Or, perhaps better said, "Give yourself room to be average." Once in a while. But don't get too comfortable delivering sub-par messages. Go for the best. You are doing the finest work in the universe and it deserves the best you can offer.

Two. As sharp as you are and as knowledgeable about your own preaching as you have become, sometimes the sermon you think bombed was more effective than you know. Case in point….

A pastor friend felt that way about last Sunday's sermon. His wife was out of town, he told me, and so there was no one readily at hand to allay his fears about the message he had delivered. He was feeling pretty low about it until two things happened. A church member called him the next day to say, "Pastor, I used your message yesterday and led a fellow to faith in Christ this morning!"

And the next day he received a note from a family who had been visiting in the services. "We felt everything in Sunday's service was outstanding—the music, the interview with the mission pastor, and the sermon. We have found our church!"

Music to a pastor's ears. Nothing boring about that!

And, speaking of boring. Read on...

CHAPTER TEN

How to Write Boring Articles and Preach Dull Sermons

My friends who read the title will think, "Finally, something Joe knows a little about!"

Every preacher, I imagine, knows about dull sermons. Anyone charged with turning out multiple sermons a week over decades will certainly produce his share of messages that are dead on arrival.

I'm thinking of a Christian writer of past years who turned out book after book and built a reputation as a leader/writer/professor of note. He was off the scene by the time I was thirty, so I never saw him when he was in his prime. But, repeatedly, I came away from his writings thinking, "How dull. Why was he considered such a wonder?" My quick answer is that the standards were different in the mid-20th century. Denominational publishing houses turned out books not for their sharp content or even sales figures but for reasons of their own. In a word, that writer was "safe."

So! The challenge on penning something about dull writings and boring sermons (or vice versa!) is to keep from being dull myself. But, always one for a challenge, let's see how this goes.

Recipe for articles and sermons that are DOA....

1. Spout platitudes.

Given a choice between a catchy turn of phrase and an old saying you've heard a thousand times, go for the latter. Faced with telling either something exciting you saw yesterday or an uninteresting rehashing of something Charles Spurgeon said 150 years ago, Spurgeon wins without a runoff.

Never meet a cliché you don't like. Pepper your sermons/writings with old bromides, common sayings, and everyday wisdom. Likewise, shun (like the plague?) any expression that would challenge the reader/listener to question his presumptions, analyze his ways, reconsider his beliefs.

Liven up your prose, writer! Spice up your preaching, pastor! How to do this? My suggestion is to spend time with children and teens. Listen to them, then try telling them something they will enjoy. Master that and you have it!

Note that I am not suggesting you imitate teens or children. Rather, learn from them.

2. Ignore the human element.

Forget you are writing to actual people. Give no thought to the fellow sitting before you who could be doing a thousand other things, most of them far more productive than listening to you. This is all about you rhapsodizing on some tiny theme you found of interest. Whether it helps anyone or not is their problem.

Harry Fosdick used to say no one ever comes to church wondering whatever happened to the Jebusites. (He was wrong, of course. We preachers wonder about that stuff. But no normal people do!) People come to church—and they read our articles and buy our books—looking for something to lift them from their sadness or grief or disappointment or frustration. Give them something uplifting, for Pete's sake!

3. Never ever tell a story.

Your congregation (or readers) will perk up and pay attention the moment you say, "The other day while waiting at a train crossing, I saw something amazing…." or "Recently, a friend told me what he did the day his house burned…."

People do love a good story. So, to deaden your sermon/article, to strip it of anything relevant to their lives, you will want to avoid fascinating tales and interesting biographies. Stay with principles and lessons, preachments, teachings, and insights. Give generalities, but not specifics.

Have you ever wondered why people found Jesus' sermons so endlessly fascinating? It was not just because of the miracles, I guarantee. Obviously, He knew what He was talking about since He was a native of Heaven and knew the Father personally. It's always fun to hear a distant country described by a native. But, also, He was a storyteller. (See Mark 4:34.) Since He had heard every story from the beginning of time—and was a major participant in many!—He was the ultimate Master Storyteller.

4. Forget the dark side.

If you are teaching/writing/preaching on, let's say, "Believe on the Lord Jesus Christ and thou shalt be saved," making that wonderful invitation mind-numbingly dull takes some doing, but you can pull it off. Spend your time in the meanings of the Greek words "believe" and "saved," and you'll soon have the audience snoring. And, if you can work in anything on the verb tenses of "believe" and "shalt be saved," so much the better. Only two people in your congregation/readership find that kind of detail interesting, making it a perfect recipe for dullness.

In truth, if you must bring in such insights from the original languages, do it quickly and move on!

What we're calling the "dark side" is the unspoken aspect of the teaching. This involves questions like "Why should they do that?" "What's keeping people from doing it?" "What happens if they don't do it?" That is to say, why do some not believe? What happens if they refuse to believe? How would one overcome the negative forces? And such.

God does not hesitate to shine a light on the dark side of issues. Men love darkness rather than light because their deeds are evil. He Himself knows our frame; He is mindful that we are but dust. Unless you repent you shall all likewise perish. God gave them up to a reprobate mind.

One reason of many we find Scripture endlessly fascinating is it rounds out the picture, never presenting platters of platitudes (sorry!) or plates of verbal pastries (double sorry!), but the Word also gives the sordid side of life, presents its heroes warts and all, and does not shrink from telling of the failures and embarrassments of the best people. The editors of *National Enquirer*, the *Globe*, the *Star*, and other supermarket scandal sheets got the idea first from Holy Writ.

5. Avoid all traces of humor.

Laughter awakens the spirit and stirs the flow of the juices in humans. So, to put your audience to sleep, avoid it at all costs. If you must tell something humorous that fits your message, be sure to dumb it down and sand all the sharp edges off it, remove all elements of surprise, and then apologize for doing humor so poorly.

My young family and I were having lunch in a home following the Sunday morning service. The adult son said, "Brother Joe, settle an argument mother and I are having. I say Jesus used to laugh. And mother says He didn't." From the kitchen came his mother's voice: "Well, the Bible doesn't say He laughed, pastor." Without thinking, I blurted out, "Mrs. Laney, the Bible doesn't say He went to the bathroom either, but He did!" She said, "Brother Joe!" and we all laughed.

Someone has said, "I don't know whether Jesus laughed or not. But He sure fixed me up so I could!"

6. Shun personal reminiscences.

Pause in your sermon and say, "When I was a child growing up on the farm...." and you have the undivided attention of your audience. At least you will as long as you can hold them. But the second you start boring again, they're gone.

A half-century ago, pastors would preface their reminiscences with an apology: "Pardon the personal reference." I would hear that and think, "Are you kidding? That was the most interesting part of your message!"

Most of what I am today–good and bad–has its roots in my childhood. I recall a thousand incidents and influences along the way which all flow together in memory. A teacher who taught me to love to read in the first grade, a teacher who read stories to us in the third and fourth grades, and a teacher who publicly humiliated me in the seventh grade–all are part of my inner makeup. A preacher who laughed in the pulpit when I was a child, a preacher who was born minus a funny bone in my teens, and a preacher who loved life in my young adulthood–they're here with me, too. So, when I preach, they sometimes make a cameo appearance.

7. Lose sight of the goal.

The purveyor of dullness almost always has as his goal to communicate something he finds interesting. And, when he arrives at the end of his material, he feels satisfied that he has achieved his purpose.

However, he's only halfway home.

Every sermon–and every inspirational article or book– is made up of two parts: **What** and **so what.**

The first, "What?" is the teaching material. The "So what?" is the application in which the writer or speaker drives home the lessons he has just given. The first is informational, the second instructional. Without the second, the first is just so much dead material, as fascinating as a operator's manual for a tractor.

When I stand to preach, if I plan to invite the congregation to fill the altar area for prayer at the conclusion of the sermon, I tell them up front. Somewhere toward the middle of the message, I may say again that in a few minutes "many of us will gather here and pray." Then, when we move into the public invitation, they're ready. But the times when I forget to prepare them, if I mention coming to pray only at the conclusion of the sermon, the response is minimal.

Likewise, if we are asking people to make a financial contribution to the work of the Lord, everything in the message should point toward that end. An evangelistic sermon should call people to Christ for salvation. The goal of the sermon should always be in mind.

Staying focused on what we are asking the hearers/readers to do is all important.

To move an article or sermon from the realm of the dead into the land of the living, then, means just the opposite of the points we teasingly made above. Effective pastors will:

–Speak freshly.

–Speak to people in real situations.

–Tell the occasional story, making sure it is relevant and well-told.

–Perhaps mention why some people refuse to believe this, rebel against such a wonderful teaching, and the price they pay for their refusal.

–Laugh with us. If something funny happened on your way to preach/write this and it fits, we are literally starving to know it. Always keep it under control, however, making sure the humor serves the purpose of the goal.

–Reminisce with us. What happened in your life that caused you to want to write this article or preach this subject?

–Keep in mind what you are asking your hearers/readers to do.

CHAPTER ELEVEN

Pastor, Take Care of Your People

A faithful shepherd will work to protect his sheep from wolves and other predators.

Pastors will all agree on the outside dangers to be watching for. However, among the internal dangers (I'm thinking of Acts 20:29 here), one that you might not think of is boring guest speakers.

How's that? I have two stories.

The first tells how on one occasion I determined to protect my people from a boring Bible study, and the second reveals how I learned that lesson in the first place.

David was a seminary professor whom we had invited to bring a Bible study to my congregation. He traveled several hundred miles and checked into the hotel in my town on Saturday night and we met for supper. I was excited. He was a great teacher and I knew it.

Some 10 years earlier, my wife and I first heard David do a Bible study at the state conference center. The way he grasped Paul's Epistle to the Ephesians and brought out insights from the Greek was thrilling. The following year we had him to our church for a study. He did an outstanding job and the congregation was strengthened by his ministry.

That's why I invited him to my next pastorate.

That Sunday morning, Professor David delivered a sermon on the epistle for the week. Sunday evening, we allotted him an hour and a half to begin the study in a serious way.

He was unbelievably boring.

I was surprised. This was not like him. I had wanted so badly for my people to hear him at his best.

The question was what to do. Should I bring this to his attention or not? And if so, how does one tell a distinguished seminary professor you are boring the pants off my people? How would he take it? Do I dare risk it?

If this had been the first time I'd been confronted with this dilemma, I probably would not have done anything. But I had faced the identical position a few years earlier.

As the new pastor of this same church, I was eager to bring in the best guest speakers and teachers. For the study on Acts the following January, I knew exactly whom to call: Jack, a retired pastor friend who had had great influence on my early life, and whom I knew to be an outstanding student of the Word and Bible teacher.

The study had begun on a Sunday evening, continuing nightly through Wednesday. My people arrived several hundred strong, all with their open Bibles and notebooks, ready to jot down insights from Jack's outstanding teaching.

He was terrible. One would have thought he had never read the 28 chapters of Acts. He chased all kinds of rabbits, told pointless stories, and lulled my people to sleep with empty talk. To say I was disappointed would be the understatement of the year.

Jack went on like that night after night, while the attendance kept dwindling. On the final night, there might have been fifteen people present. But Jack seemed not to notice or care. He kept right on with his pointless chatter, completely failing to teach anything remotely like the Book of Acts.

The benediction was prayed, we gave him a check, and he went on his way.

Never again, I decided.

Never again would I allow this to happen to my people without my making an attempt to salvage the occasion.

So, now, a few years later, when my invited Bible teacher begins to disappoint, I know what I'm going to do. I'm going to tell Professor David that his Bible teaching is terrible. I'm willing to risk hurting him in order not to abandon my people.

So, Monday morning, I called on him at the Holiday Inn. Inside his room, I pulled up a chair and jumped right in.

"Brother David, I need to take up a matter with you. This is very difficult for me."

He: "Well, let's have it! Get it out. What's bothering you?"

Let's just say that David was as loud and bombastic in the hotel room as he could sometimes be in his pulpit delivery. It did not make my task any easier.

I said, "My friend, I've heard you teach the Word. There is no one better in the world. You are an excellent Bible teacher."

Nothing from him. He knows I'm about to drop the other shoe.

"But you are not doing it here," I said. "In fact, you have bored my people to tears."

"With anyone else," I continued, "I'd probably let it go. But I know what you are capable of. You know how to open the Word and show what it says and what it means. You are able to tell us the Greek that reveals so much of the content we had not seen before."

He interrupted. "Oh! You want me to impress them with my knowledge of the Greek?!! I can do that, if that's the problem!!"

I said softly, "No, sir. That is not what I'm asking for. I want you to open the Word of God and teach them.

And where you have an insight from the original language that would bless them, share it."

He was quiet. I said, "I'm just telling you that these people are sharp. They are good Bible students. And they love to be fed spiritual red meat. So, I want you to put it out there."

Give him credit. He did. And I never heard another word out of him in private about our little confrontation.

Paul told the elders of the Ephesian church, I *know this…savage wolves will come in among you, not sparing the flock. Also, from among yourselves men will rise up, speaking perverse things, to draw away the disciples after themselves. Therefore, watch.* (Acts 20:29-31)

Watch for the wolves from outside, pastor.

Furthermore, watch for the enemy to rise up from among the congregation too. Killers can arise from either area.

And, while you're at it, watch out also for those who would kill the sheep by simply boring them to death.

Sometimes the best people can do the worst work.

Help them out.

Do your favorite Bible teacher a favor when you decide he is insulting the intelligence of your people.

Tell him to turn it up a notch. Tell him to feed the sheep, and not sedate them.

As a young pastor, when invited by a pastor friend for a weeklong meeting, I was excited but anxious. I wanted so much to preach sermons that would feed the flock and give guidance to the unsaved that sometimes I overburdened myself with worry. As a result, my sermons were often woefully lacking.

Pastor Howard Taylor, my host at Calvary, Greenville, MS, did me a favor. After hearing a couple of my sermons, he came by the hotel for a brief visit. "Joe," he said, "may I make a suggestion about your preaching?"

"I would welcome any help you can give me," I told him.

"Preach for decisions," he said.

That's all he said.

I knew immediately what he was saying. I was giving good information, was probably being used of the Lord to bless some people, and may have even been entertaining one or two. But the point of an evangelistic meeting is to encourage people to give their lives to Christ. My job as the visiting preacher was to urge them to do that, to give them good reasons and proper motivation, and to call on them to make this commitment.

It takes courage to give a rebuke, gentle or not, to the visiting preacher. But far better to risk offending him than to abandon your people.

As pastor, I have a far greater debt to my congregation than to any visiting preacher.

CHAPTER TWELVE

Someone Is Always on Deck, Pastor.

In a baseball game, the batter stands at the plate, ready to swing at the ball. Not far away and off to one side, another batter is standing, bat on his shoulder, waiting his turn.

They say he is "on deck."

Someone else is always on deck.

Windy Rich spent the last decades of his outstanding ministry serving churches as interim minister of education. He provided invaluable help to two churches I served. Always, as he arrived to begin his ministry for a few months, Windy would announce, "I have come to leave."

He had no plans to work this into something permanent and wanted no one to be threatened about the loss of their position.

I told Windy that while I liked that statement, "There is a sense that it applies to all of us. Every one of us has come to leave."

Pastors and staff may stay fifteen years or two years. But we all leave, and when we do, someone else will come behind us.

It's a wise pastor who leads a church with his successors in mind.

A suggestion or two to every pastor--

One. Even though they call you the "permanent" pastor, don't let it fool you. We're all on temporary assignment for the Master. One day you will leave and someone else will occupy the office you have come to love and preach to your people. Get used to it.

Two. So, treat your calling to this congregation with that in mind. Honor Christ. Love these people. Build for the future. Lay a solid foundation for long-term health and effective ministry.

Three. Help your people to see themselves not as a kingdom unto themselves but as one part of the whole Body of Christ. They are part of the church down the street and the ones across town. In one church I served, we would list a local church and its pastor in our Sunday bulletin and pray for them in the service. Sometimes, the deacon of the week would phone that church to see if they had specific prayer requests. To our shame, that kind of "loving one another" is rare, but is so welcome and so needed.

Four. As pastor, you should honor the ministers who followed you in previous churches and then, honor the Lord's servant who will follow you here.

"It is the Lord Christ we serve," says the Word.

Five. When the time comes for you to move on--to another church or position or into retirement--don't dilly dally. Get on with it.

Move out and get out of the way so the next person can do the work the Father has planned. We've all known preachers who overstayed their welcome. I suspect they had become possessive about their positions and territorial in their work. "This is my church." Such a sad mistake. It isn't. Never was. Jesus cleared that up.

"I will build My church," He said (Matthew 16:18). It's His church. He died for it, you didn't.

I tell pastors and other church leaders they would be amazed how liberating it is to take hands off the Lord's church and give it back to Him. Thereafter, the only question they face is "Lord, what do You want us to do today with Your church?"

Let us go forth to bless Him in His church.

Final Words

Preaching the Word, pastoring the Lord's people, serving the Lord Jesus Christ--this is the absolutely greatest work in the world. It's eternal, it's real world stuff, it's righteous.

But it can be hard, discouraging, and dangerous even. (Read Matthew 10:16-42 if you need a reminder.)

We all need all the help we can get. We need frequent reminders, constant motivating, the stimulation of friends, and fresh input from reading and studying all the time. Staleness is a never-ending threat.

Always, we need to be encouraging one another in the work.

"Do not grow weary in well doing," friend. "In due season, we shall reap---if we don't quit."

Don't quit.

About the Author

Joe McKeever is a native of rural Alabama, the son of a coal miner who married a farmer's daughter. Joe has been preaching for nearly 60 years. He has degrees from Birmingham-Southern College and New Orleans Baptist Theological Seminary. He pastored the First Baptist Churches of Columbus, Mississippi, Charlotte, North Carolina, and Kenner, Louisiana. He served five years as Director of Missions for the SBC churches in metro New Orleans. He and his wife Bertha have written books on "Grief Recovery 101" and "Sixty and Better: Making the Most of Our Golden Years." Joe also has written "Help! I'm a Deacon."

He is a lifelong cartoonist who has drawn for religious publications for fifty years. These days he does a daily cartoon for the Baptist Press (www.bpnews.net), illustrates books, and sketches thousands of people a year in churches, schools, and conventions. Joe has been writing for his blog (www.joemckeever.com) for fifteen years, articles directed toward pastors and other church leaders.

www.ingramcontent.com/pod-product-compliance
Lightning Source LLC
Chambersburg PA
CBHW052202110526
44591CB00012B/2042